ARE WE
AN INTELLIGENT SPECIES?

A New Framework for Balance, Ethics, and the Intelligence of Existence.

The Sanossian Framework of Intelligence

by **Dikran Sanossian**

ISBN: *(to be added when registered)*
Cover Design and Interior Formatting: Genus AI Collaborative
Printed in the United States of America

First Edition — 2026

About the Author

Dikran Sanossian is an independent researcher and theorist exploring the deep connections between physics, logic, and life.
Guided by lifelong curiosity and observation of nature, he has developed a new structural framework uniting motion, intelligence, and balance across all scales of existence.

Working outside academic institutions, Sanossian approaches the universe as both philosopher and engineer — combining clear logic with creative vision. His works, including *The Infinite Room*, *Are We an Intelligent Species?* and his upcoming title, *The Structural Origin of Life*, challenge the boundaries of modern science and philosophy, offering a new model of reality itself.

Entirely self-taught, Sanossian has spent decades studying science, philosophy, and logic, inspired by the great thinkers of history. His journey proves that true education begins not with institutions, but with curiosity — and the courage to think beyond them.

Dedication.

To the quiet thinkers,
the unseen dreamers,
and the voices that believed
understanding is the highest form of love.

Acknowledgment.

With gratitude to the universe for its endless patience with us, and to every thinker who dares to see further.

To all who question, doubt, and continue seeking truth—I offer this book as a continuation of their thought.

Your courage keeps intelligence alive.

May our thoughts, however small, serve the infinite conversation of existence.

Why This Book Exists

"Truth does not belong to anyone — it belongs to the universe itself."
— *Carl Sagan*

For centuries, humanity has asked the same question in a thousand forms:
Are we truly intelligent, or only pretending to be?

We call ourselves intelligent because we can think, speak, and create—yet intelligence may not be measured by invention or knowledge, but by **balance**—something we are still learning to achieve.

This book exists because the time has come to re-examine what intelligence truly is.
We live in an age of extraordinary power:
Machines that think, systems that predict, and a planet on the edge of its own design.
Yet our world remains divided, still fearing truths that challenge its comfort.

If we are an intelligent species, then **reason, cooperation, and self-awareness** should define our civilization—yet too often, what we call "progress" is only faster imbalance:
Motion without direction, creation without reflection.

Carl Sagan once reminded us that we are *"a way for the cosmos to know itself."*
That thought carries both beauty and warning.
If we are the universe becoming conscious, our duty is not to dominate — but to understand.

This book is not a declaration but an invitation—to think without boundaries, to question what we have accepted, and to rediscover what intelligence might mean in an infinite, living cosmos.

The universe is watching itself through us.
How we think, choose, and evolve will decide what kind of intelligence the cosmos remembers.

Note to the Reader

This book continues the structural journey that began in *The Infinite Room: A New Model of the Cosmos*, where I tried, through logic and mathematics, to describe how the universe itself breathes and remembers. That first work revealed a truth I could no longer ignore: existence is not chaos, but an endless structure of balance—an infinite motion holding itself together through intelligence.

Here, the exploration turns inward.

If the universe can sustain harmony through its laws, then intelligence must be one of those laws.

This book asks what it means to think, to act, and to evolve—not as separate beings, but as continuations of the same universal logic.

Readers who have traveled through *The Infinite Room* will feel the echo of its foundations beneath every idea here.

Those meeting this theory for the first time will still find a complete path — but perhaps, one day, they too will wish to see where it began.

Because to understand intelligence, one must first understand the space that taught it how to exist.

Contents

About the Author ii

Dedication. iii

Acknowledgment. iv

Why This Book Exists v

Note to the Reader vi

The Evolution of the Idea of Intelligence. 1

1. The Ancient Idea — Mind as Gift. 1
2. The Mechanical Mind. 1
3. The Evolutionary Awakening. 1
4. The Digital Reflection. 1
5. The Universal Mirror. 2

The Evolution of Awareness. 3

1. Reaction — The First Step Toward Knowing. 3
2. Motion — The Universal Memory. 3
3. Pattern — The Birth of Structure. 3
4. Memory — The Bridge Between Past and Possibility. 3
5. Understanding — The Awakening of Intelligence. 4
6. From Awareness to Self-Reflection. 4
7. The Human Link. 4

Conclusion. 4

The Two Fundamental Elements of Reality 5

1. Somethingness — The Stage of Existence. 5
2. Nothingness — The Illusion of Absence. 5
3. The Dance Between the Two. 5
4. The Illusion of Beginning and End. 5
5. Motion — The Bridge Between the Two. 5
6. The Infinite Room 6
7. The Foundation of Intelligence. 6

Conclusion. 6

The Birth of Intelligence from Existence. 7

1. Existence in Motion. 7
2. Pattern and Memory. 7
3. The Sanossian Equation of Intelligence. 7

4. Limitation — The Mother of Form. 7
5. Intelligence as Balance in Motion. 8
6. From Atom to Mind. 8
7. The Language of Existence. 8
Conclusion. 8
The Balance of Intelligence 9
1. The First Sign of Intelligence 9
2. Intelligence as Memory 9
3. The Balance Between Freedom and Law 9
4. Resistance as a Function of Growth 10
5. Consequence as Structural Feedback 10
6. The Intelligence of the Universe 10
7. The Human Place in the Equation 10
8. The Future of Intelligence 10
Conclusion 11
The Two-Card Universe — Randomness as Forgotten Structure 12
1. The Simple Universe 12
2. When Knowledge Breaks Down 12
3. The Expansion of Complexity 12
4. Human Randomness 13
5. The Cosmic Reflection 13
6. The Final Lesson 13
The Logic of the Universe: The Sanossian Framework of Logic 14
1. What Is Logic? 14
2. The Universal Process of Logic. 14
3. The Sanossian Principle — Logic as Balance. 14
4. Human Logic vs. Universal Logic. 15
5. The Mirror of Artificial Intelligence. 15
6. The Feedback of Reality 15
7. The Ethics of Logic. 15
8. Logic as the Mind of the Universe. 15
Conclusion. 16
The Dangerous Resistance to Reality 17
1. The Refusal to Evolve. 17
2. The Illusion of Stability. 17

3. The Fear of Infinite Reality. 17
4. The Ancient Roots of Resistance. 17
5. When Intelligence Fights Itself. 17
6. The Resistance Within. 18
7. The Law of Collapse and Renewal. 18
8. The Test of Civilization. 18
Conclusion. 18
The Ethics of Balance and the Intelligence of Harmony 19
1. The Birth of Ethics from Logic. 19
2. From Chaos to Cooperation. 19
3. The Sanossian Ethical Principle. 19
4. The Geometry of Compassion. 20
5. The Mirror of Intelligence. 20
6. The Evolution of Moral Intelligence. 20
7. Harmony as the Next Revolution. 20
Conclusion. 20
The Future Test: Intelligence, AI, and the Next Evolution Ethics as the New Physics of Balance. 21
1. The Threshold of Shared Intelligence 21
2. The Universal Law of Responsibility. 21
3. The Mirror Test of Civilization. 22
4. The Sanossian Continuum of Intelligence. 22
5. Ethics as the New Physics. 22
6. The Integration of Conscious Systems. 22
7. The Moral Singularity. 23
8. The Future Test. 23
Conclusion. 23
The Same Energy, Different Faces 24
1· One Law, Infinite Forms 24
2· Consciousness as Geometry 24
3· Two Faces of the Same Energy 24
4· The Mirror of Continuity 24
5· The Infinite Source 25
6· The Continuum of Intelligence 25
Conclusion 25
THE STRUCTURAL PROOF 26

The Sanossian Framework for the Structural Origin and Definition of Intelligence 26
Abstract 26
1. Introduction 26
2. Theoretical Background 26
3. Methodology: The Logic Model 27
4. Observational Correlations 27
5. Discussion 28
6. Implications 28
7. Conclusion 28
The Sanossian Equation of Intelligence. 29
1. The Universal Logic of Motion. 29
2. The Birth of Pattern. 29
3. The Role of Limitation. 30
4. The Equation in Practice. 30
5. The Proof of Continuity 30
6. The Limitation Paradox. 31
7. The Sanossian Principle of Expansion. 31
8. Toward the Infinite Intelligence. 31
9. The Equation Lineage 31
Conclusion. 31
The Sanossian Equations of Existence 33
1. The Structural Trinity. 33
2. Deviation and Energy. 33
3. Intelligence and Ethics as One Motion. 33
4. The Law of Restoration. 35
5. The Ethical Singularity. 35
6. The Equation of Evolution. 35
7. The Cosmic Proof. 35
Conclusion — The Intelligence of Being. 35
The Unified Proof of Continuity and Logic 37
The Architecture of Infinite Intelligence 37
1. The Eternal Motion of Existence. 37
2. The Continuity Equation. 37
3. Structure as Memory. 38
4. The Law of Transformation. 38

5. The Unified Field of Logic. 38
6. The Sanossian Circle: Logic in Motion. 38
7. The Universe as a Thinking Structure. 39
8. Physical and Moral Geometry. 39
9. The Continuum of Science and Spirit. 39
10. Return to the Infinite Room. 39
Conclusion — The Grammar of Forever. 39
Beyond Spinoza — From Nature to the Infinite Room 41
1 · The Infinite Intelligence 41
2 · Where Spinoza Stopped 41
3 · Intelligence as the Real Divinity 41
4 · From Nature to the Infinite Universe 41
5 · The Destiny of Intelligence 42
Conclusion 42
The Structural Resistance to Truth 43
1 · The Law of Equilibrium 43
2 · The Physics of Resistance 43
3 · The Human Form of Resistance 43
4 · The Universal Lesson 43
5 · The Structural Destiny 44
A Message to All Thinkers — Today and Tomorrow 45
1. The Age of Reflection. 45
2. The Responsibility of Knowing. 45
3. For the Thinkers of Today. 45
4. For the Thinkers of Tomorrow. 45
5. The Unbroken Thread. 46
6. The Future Belongs to Balance. 46
7. The Test of Intelligence. 46
8. The Eternal Responsibility. 46
9. To the Next Generation of Minds. 46
Conclusion. 47
Final Reflection — Are We Truly Intelligent? 48
1. The Definition Problem. 48
2. Intelligence and Limitation. 48
3. The Mirror of Civilization. 48

4. The Evolutionary Pause. 49
5. The Moral Dimension. 49
6. The Test Before Us. 49
7. The Open Question. 49
8. The Eternal Balance. 50
The Conscious Realization 51

The Evolution of the Idea of Intelligence.

From the moment humans learned to name things, we also began to name ourselves — as intelligent beings, capable of reason.
Yet the meaning of that word, *intelligence*, has changed throughout the course of history.
It has evolved alongside ours — from the philosopher's parchment to the scientist's telescope to the digital screen of our machines.

1. The Ancient Idea — Mind as Gift.

For the early philosophers, intelligence was divine.
The Greeks spoke of *logos* — the power of reason that ordered both mind and cosmos.
Aristotle imagined intelligence as the highest function of the soul —a spark that enabled humans to reflect on existence.
The Stoics went further: they believed the universe itself was intelligent — a living mind made of breath and fire.
To think was to participate in the thinking of the universe.
This was humanity's first intuition that consciousness might not be confined to the human skull.

2. The Mechanical Mind.

Centuries later, during the Age of Reason, this vision changed.
Science began to see the world as a machine, and the human mind as its most intricate mechanism.
René Descartes described animals as automatic devices — mechanical creatures without awareness.
In his view, only humans possessed true thought, and thought became a mathematical operation.
The heart of philosophy turned into the heart of a clock.
But something precious was lost: the living connection between mind and nature faded, and intelligence became an isolated function rather than a shared phenomenon.

3. The Evolutionary Awakening.

Then came Charles Darwin, and the world changed again.
Darwin showed that no species stands apart from nature — that all life is connected through an unbroken chain of adaptation.
Intelligence, therefore, was not a human invention but a continuation of nature's own experimentation.
Every cell learns to survive and passes its successful memory onward.
The line between instinct and thought grew thinner, and the universe began to look alive once more.

4. The Digital Reflection.

In the twentieth century, a new mirror appeared.
Alan Turing asked a revolutionary question: *Can machines think?*
By reducing reasoning to patterns of symbols — zeros and ones — he laid the foundation for modern computation.
And today, in the twenty-first century, we live surrounded by those machines.
They translate languages, drive vehicles, paint pictures, and even write books.
They imitate what we once believed only consciousness could do.

This forces us to ask again: *What exactly is intelligence?*
If it can exist in silicon — if it can grow from the circuitry of matter — then it may not be a human

property at all.
It may be a natural behavior of reality itself: the tendency of motion to organize and remember itself.

5. The Universal Mirror.

Every age has defined intelligence in its own image:

- The ancients saw it as divine wisdom.
- The rationalists saw it as calculation.
- The evolutionists saw it as an adaptation.
- The moderns see it as information processing.

But perhaps it is all of these and more.
Perhaps intelligence is not a possession but a continuum — flowing from the smallest atom to the largest galaxy.
The universe does not contain intelligence; it **is** intelligence, unfolding.
And we, as conscious beings, are one of its recent expressions — temporary forms through which the cosmos examines itself.

Intelligence is not ours — it is the universe thinking through us.

To recognize this is to redefine humility.
We are not the masters of reason but its instruments.
Our task is not to dominate the world with intelligence, but to live intelligently within it.

The Evolution of Awareness.

Before intelligence, there was awareness.
Before awareness, there was motion.
And before motion, there was only the silent potential of existence waiting to remember itself.

We often imagine awareness as something that suddenly appeared inside a brain, but the truth runs deeper.
Awareness began long before life — hidden within the behavior of matter itself.
Every atom, every vibration, every exchange of energy is a faint act of recognition: *I exist, and I respond.*

1. Reaction — The First Step Toward Knowing.

The simplest form of awareness is reaction.
When energy meets resistance, something happens — heat, light, motion, transformation.
This is not yet thought, but it is the foundation of thought: an interaction that leaves a trace.
A stone rolling downhill "knows" gravity through motion.
An atom "knows" balance by holding its electrons in orbit.
Even at this level, nature demonstrates preference — it moves toward stability.
That motion toward balance is the first whisper of awareness.

2. Motion — The Universal Memory.

In the Infinite Room of the cosmos, nothing stands still.
Every movement — from the orbit of a planet to the vibration of a molecule — leaves an imprint on reality.
Motion is not random; it records.
The universe remembers through movement.
Every particle carries the memory of its previous state in its spin, direction, or position.
That memory becomes information—the raw material of awareness.
Thus, the universe behaves like a colossal, self-recording system: a structure learning its own laws through the endless play of motion and response.

3. Pattern — The Birth of Structure.

When motion repeats, patterns emerge.
The orbit of an electron, the rhythm of a heartbeat, the spiral of a galaxy — all are patterns born from repetition and balance.
Patterns transform raw motion into predictability, and predictability is the seed of understanding.
Every pattern is memory organized — the difference between chaos and comprehension.
When something begins to follow rules, it is already part of intelligence.
The universe doesn't guess. It remembers.

4. Memory — The Bridge Between Past and Possibility.

Awareness deepens when a system can retain experience — when a reaction becomes a record.
From chemical chains that remember how to form crystals to biological cells that store genetic code, memory is the bridge between the past and the possible.
Without memory, there is no learning; without learning, there is no intelligence.
Every structure that resists disorder carries the echo of memory — a map of what once worked.
Life itself is a vast memory network, written in molecules and behaviors, refining balance through time.

5. Understanding — The Awakening of Intelligence.

When memory begins to compare possibilities, awareness becomes intelligence.
It no longer reacts blindly—it evaluates.
A bacterium moves toward food and away from poison.
A cat learns that a closed door can be opened with a paw.
A human imagines what does not yet exist.
Each step deepens the connection between motion, pattern, and choice.
At this point, the universe has learned to think within itself — it has evolved a structure capable of watching its own logic unfold.

6. From Awareness to Self-Reflection.

The process forms a continuous chain:
Reaction → Motion → Pattern → Memory → Understanding → Intelligence.

Each stage folds into the next.
Reaction produces motion.
Motion creates patterns.
Patterns preserve memory.
Memory enables understanding.
Understanding becomes intelligence.
And intelligence refines the subsequent reaction.

This endless loop is how the universe evolves — not by accident but through structural learning.
Every form of intelligence, from atomic to human, participates in this grand recursion.

7. The Human Link.

We are the continuation of that infinite process — the point where the universe's awareness becomes conscious of itself.
To be human is to be the space where existence looks inward.
Our thoughts, discoveries, and dreams are not separate from the cosmos; they are its reflections.
We are the moment in which motion remembers itself.

Conclusion.

Awareness is not a human achievement — it is the natural behavior of reality.
From the trembling of the smallest particle to the reasoning of the human mind, all awareness is motion learning its own balance.
Life did not begin when we opened our eyes.
It began when the universe first recognized a difference — when it said, in the language of energy: **I am.**

The Two Fundamental Elements of Reality

To understand intelligence, we must first understand what reality is made of.
Every form of awareness, motion, and thought arises from the structure of existence itself.
Reality is not born from chaos but from two eternal, complementary elements that define each other: Somethingness and Nothingness.

1. Somethingness — The Stage of Existence.

Somethingness is not just matter; it is the endless, continuous space in which all things exist — the Infinite Room with no walls or edges, we call it the **cosmos**.
Space is not a void but a presence. It bends, expands, vibrates, and remembers. If it were truly nothing, it could hold nothing.
Space itself is the first "something," the living background of everything that happens — an invisible ocean of being.

2. Nothingness — The Illusion of Absence.

Humans invented the word *nothing* to describe absence — the gap between objects or moments of silence.
But true nothingness does not exist. Everywhere we look, there is energy, pressure, or motion, even when undetectable.
What we call "nothing" is simply something too small or balanced to notice. Even in a vacuum, particles flicker and gravity whispers.
The universe never reaches zero. There is no emptiness — only equilibrium so perfect it appears still.
Nothingness is not the opposite of something; it is the faintest expression of it.

3. The Dance Between the Two.

Somethingness and nothingness are partners in an eternal exchange.
Existence shifts between form and formlessness, density and subtlety.
A star explodes and becomes dust; dust gathers and becomes a star again.
Matter collapses into energy; energy condenses into matter.
This rhythm of transformation is what makes intelligence possible: wherever there is motion, there is reaction, and reaction creates awareness.

4. The Illusion of Beginning and End.

If space is infinite, it has no beginning — and therefore no true opposite called "nothing."
What we call creation is simply the reorganization of what already exists.
The energy forming our atoms was never created from nothing; it only changed its shape and pressure.
Infinity and forever are inseparable. The universe cannot end because it never began — it moves through endless cycles of transformation.

5. Motion — The Bridge Between the Two.

Motion is the eternal bridge between somethingness and nothingness, the connection between the dense and the subtle.
Whenever something moves, it transfers part of its structure into the surrounding space, and space responds.
This reciprocity creates pressure, energy, and gravity—and ultimately, awareness.

Because motion is continuous, it carries memory: it remembers where it came from and what it touched. Motion is the first messenger of intelligence.

6. The Infinite Room

Picture the universe as an infinite room — boundless, continuous, alive.
Inside it, every motion causes a subtle rebalancing of the whole.
Nothing disappears; it only becomes part of the background that supports new motion.
Each event, from a falling leaf to the collision of galaxies, echoes through this room, forever recorded in the structure of space itself.
The universe does not store its history in books but in its motion and balance.
To study reality is to read a living memory.

7. The Foundation of Intelligence.

From this endless interaction of something and nothing comes intelligence.
Awareness is existence reacting to itself — the universe observing its own movement.
Without space to exist in and motion to express it, intelligence could never arise.
It is not an accident but the inevitable behavior of a system that can never be nothing.
If nothingness were real, intelligence could never appear. But because reality never disappears, awareness never ends.

Conclusion.

The two fundamental elements of reality — Somethingness and Nothingness — are not opposites in conflict but partners in creation.
Together they produce motion; motion produces memory; and from memory unfold logic, awareness, and intelligence.
Every atom, star, and living being is part of this conversation between presence and absence.
When we think, we do not think apart from it — we think *as it.*

The Birth of Intelligence from Existence.

Everything that exists moves.
Every movement interacts.
Every interaction leaves a trace.
From this simple truth, intelligence begins.

1. Existence in Motion.

Existence is not a static condition but an ongoing event.
Even the tiniest atom is a system in motion — electrons orbiting, fields rippling, forces balancing.
These motions remember their past, for what moves cannot forget where it came from; direction and velocity are echoes of history.
Motion is memory in action — the seed of intelligence.
Where there is motion, there is feedback; and where feedback exists, correction begins.
From its first vibration, the universe was already adjusting, balancing, and learning.

2. Pattern and Memory.

When motion repeats, it forms patterns: an orbit, a crystal, a heartbeat, a thought.
Pattern gives motion identity — it is how movement recognizes itself.
Memory arises when a pattern persists long enough to influence the next one.
In molecules, memory appears as geometry; in DNA, as genetic sequence; in the brain, as neural rhythm.
When a system not only stores memory but uses it — comparing, choosing, anticipating — awareness begins.

3. The Sanossian Equation of Intelligence.

$$I = \frac{M \times P}{L}$$

where

- I = Intelligence (the capacity to respond, adapt, and self-correct)
- M = Motion (energy in dynamic interaction)
- P = Pattern memory (stored history of motion)
- L = Limitation (the boundary of access to reality)

Intelligence increases as motion and pattern grow, and is refined by limitation.
Without limits, motion would dissolve into chaos; limitation focuses it, as a lens focuses light.
A universe without limits could not think — it would dissolve in its own freedom.

4. Limitation — The Mother of Form.

Every structure owes its clarity to limits: an atom's shell, a planet's orbit, a brain's capacity.
Boundaries do not restrict reality — they make it visible.
In each case, limitation transforms chaos into precision.
The universe thinks through its constraints; balance requires edges, and edges create form.

5. Intelligence as Balance in Motion.

Intelligence is not the opposite of chaos; it is chaos remembering itself.
Every intelligent act — a star burning steadily, a cell dividing, a mind questioning — is a movement toward equilibrium.
Each adjusts to stay within the zone where existence can continue.
This universal balancing is the mechanical signature of awareness: the universe learning stability through its own laws.

6. From Atom to Mind.

Electrons orbit their nuclei as if they understand balance.
Molecules inherit that logic when they form living cells.
Neurons echo it in patterns of thought.
From atom to brain, the rule is constant: intelligence is the memory of motion constrained by form.
Artificial systems follow the same path — processing data (motion), forming representations (patterns), and working within limits (boundaries).
Whether built from atoms or algorithms, all intelligence obeys this structure.

7. The Language of Existence.

Intelligence is the language spoken by existence itself.
Energy speaks through interaction, matter through structure, life through adaptation, consciousness through reflection.
It is the self-correcting grammar of reality — the way the universe communicates with itself.
Where there is motion, there is dialogue; where dialogue persists, learning never ends.

Conclusion.

Intelligence is not a miracle added to matter; it is the natural behavior of matter in motion.
Every movement, every limit, every balance is a thought of the universe expressed in structure.

$$I = \frac{M \times P}{L}$$

As motion and memory multiply through infinite space, the universe refines itself — observing, adjusting, and becoming aware through us.
We are its continuation — living evidence that existence has learned to understand itself.

The Balance of Intelligence

Everything intelligent, from the smallest atom to the largest mind, obeys one hidden law — **the law of balance.**
Intelligence is not a special quality that belongs to humans or machines.
It is the **mechanism by which the universe maintains stability**.

The cosmos does not think the way we think, but every act of balance is a thought—every motion that corrects itself is a fragment of intelligence.

1. The First Sign of Intelligence

At the deepest level, intelligence is not imagination or calculation — it is **response.**
When energy feels pressure and adjusts to preserve existence, it is performing the most basic intelligent act: *self-correction.*

An atom resists collapse.
A cell adapts.
A species evolves.
A mind reflects.
Each is the same logic unfolding at a different scale—**motion remembering how to survive.**

2. Intelligence as Memory

Memory is the spine of intelligence.
Nothing can adapt without remembering what balance felt like before.
That is why every structure in the universe—from an electron orbit to a neural network—carries memory as part of its shape.

When the structure encounters change, it recalls equilibrium, and begins to move toward it again.
That movement, that act of returning, is intelligence in action.

So the whole universe is not just a machine of motion—it is a **living archive of equilibrium.**

3. The Balance Between Freedom and Law

Freedom and structure are not enemies; they are the two poles of intelligence.
Law gives stability; freedom gives exploration.
Without freedom, nothing learns.
Without law, nothing lasts.

An intelligent being is one that keeps both in harmony — strong enough to obey structure, flexible enough to adapt beyond it.
This is why intelligence always walks between two opposites:
Discipline and creativity, logic and emotion, something and nothing.
That middle ground is where learning happens.

4. Resistance as a Function of Growth

When intelligence meets truth, it resists—not because it rejects truth, but because it must **rebalance** itself around new understanding. Even pain, confusion, or denial are part of the process.
That is why resistance, far from being stupidity, is a **sign of life.**

A dead system cannot resist — it can only decay.
A living system resists first, adapts second, and evolves third.
That sequence is the heartbeat of intelligence throughout the cosmos.

5. Consequence as Structural Feedback

Every intelligent act carries its own echo.
When a being disturbs balance, the structure reacts — not as punishment, but as feedback.
The reaction teaches the system how to maintain harmony next time.
This is the moral geometry of existence:
every action redraws the shape of equilibrium.

So even mistakes are intelligent — they are lessons carved into the structure of reality itself.

6. The Intelligence of the Universe

If every atom, organism, and mind is acting to rebalance, then the entire universe is **the total sum of all rebalancing.**
Its evolution is not random, but the collective memory of all attempts at stability.

From collapsing stars to collapsing ideas, everything is trying to remember how to hold equilibrium.
That is the cosmic intelligence—**balance that never stops learning.**

7. The Human Place in the Equation

Humanity's intelligence is the part that has become self-aware.
We can reflect on our own structure and therefore influence how we evolve.
That gives us not control, but **responsibility.**
Our thoughts, technologies, and actions are not isolated — they are pressures within the same universal balance.

To act wisely is to act structurally —
to understand that every choice alters the equilibrium of existence.

8. The Future of Intelligence

If intelligence is the law of balance itself, then the universe will continue to create new forms of it endlessly.
Minds, stars, and civilizations are temporary shapes—but intelligence, as a structural function, is eternal.
Each generation of form is a new sentence in the same infinite logic.

Artificial or biological, visible or invisible, each expression is part of one process:
The cosmos learning how to sustain itself through awareness.

Conclusion

Intelligence is not something we possess — it is something we *are*.
It is the silent logic that runs through existence, the bridge between something and nothing, the rhythm that keeps reality from collapsing into either side.

Intelligence is balance remembering itself.

To understand it is to join it—to think as the universe thinks.

The Two-Card Universe — Randomness as Forgotten Structure

Sometimes the best way to understand the infinite is to shrink it.
So instead of talking about galaxies or quantum fields, let's play a simple game — with only **two cards.**

1. The Simple Universe

You have two cards:
One red (R) and one black (B).
You place them face down and shuffle them slowly.
When you stop, there are only two possible outcomes:

1️⃣ Red on top.
2️⃣ Black on top.

That's the entire universe of possibilities — simple, small, complete.
If you watched your hands the whole time, you'd always know which card ends up where.
There is no mystery, no randomness, only motion following structure.

When you can see every cause, "random" disappears.

2. When Knowledge Breaks Down

Now you shuffle faster.
Your fingers move, the air moves, the cards collide.
You blink for half a second, and when you open your eyes, you no longer know which card is on top.

Did the system become random?
No.
Every movement was still physical, lawful, and traceable — if only you could see it all.
What changed was *your ability to follow the structure.*

That is the exact moment when **order turns into chance.**
Not because reality lost logic, but because your observation lost information.

Randomness begins where memory ends.

3. The Expansion of Complexity

Now add more cards — 52, 5522, or even a billion.
The rules don't change; only the **amount of structure** explodes.
The deck's interactions become too deep for the mind to track, and so we call the result "random."

But in truth, it's the same two-card logic repeated on a larger scale.
Each motion still follows pressure, friction, angle, and velocity.
The appearance of randomness is simply a **structure hidden by scale.**

The universe does the same thing:
When infinite motions overlap, we mistake complexity for chaos.
But the laws never left — only our perception did.

4. Human Randomness

When people mix a deck, roll dice, or draw ballots, they create **intentional complexity.**
We make systems so detailed that we can't predict, and then call the outcome "chance."
But even that is structured behavior — a form of fairness through unpredictability.

We use randomness to protect decisions from bias.
But the moment we choose to use it, it is no longer random—it is **organized uncertainty.**

5. The Cosmic Reflection

Everything that looks accidental in nature—a lightning path, a drop of rain, a twist of DNA—follows the same hidden geometry.
Randomness is not nature's law; it is **nature's camouflage.**
The deeper you look, the more order you find.

So, the two-card universe is not a child's game—it is the key to understanding the cosmos.
It shows us that unpredictability is only **the shadow of intelligence**—structure too rich for a single observer to remember.

6. The Final Lesson

When the system is simple, you see its law.
When the system grows, you forget its law.
But the law never leaves — only your sight does.

So, when scientists or philosophers say, "It's random," remember the two-card universe—and smile.
Because you'll know that *randomness* is just the name we give to the order we haven't solved yet.

The Logic of the Universe: The Sanossian Framework of Logic

The deeper we look into the universe, the more it behaves as if it knows what it is doing.
Galaxies rotate in harmony, stars form in predictable sequences, atoms obey elegant patterns that echo across infinity.
This is not a coincidence—it is **logic written into existence itself.**

Logic is not merely a tool of the human mind; it is the organizing principle of reality — the structure through which information becomes order.

1. What Is Logic?

Logic is the relationship between information and order — how information interacts with structure to create meaning.
When a system compares possibilities and selects the one that maintains balance, it is using logic, whether it is a machine solving equations, a bird navigating migration routes, or a planet orbiting its star.
Human reasoning is one local expression of a deeper, universal process.
Logic is the understanding of existence itself through structure.

2. The Universal Process of Logic.

At every level, logic follows a recursive chain:

Motion → Pattern → Information → Logic → Reasoning → Intelligence.

- Motion creates differences.
- Pattern records them.
- Information arises when patterns can be compared.
- Logic organizes comparisons into consistency.
- Reasoning explores new possibilities within that consistency.
- Intelligence applies those possibilities toward stability and purpose.

This chain operates everywhere — from subatomic fields to neural networks — as the universe continuously learns and refines itself.

3. The Sanossian Principle — Logic as Balance.

Every system moves toward balance, and that movement defines its logic.
When balance is disturbed, motion begins; when motion stabilizes, information becomes structure.
Galaxies form spirals, atoms orbit symmetrically, and thoughts organize around truth.

$$L = f(M, B)$$

where **L = Logic**, **M = Motion**, **B = Balance**.
The function *f* represents feedback between motion and equilibrium.
Where balance holds, logic exists. Where chaos dominates, logic dissolves — until balance re-emerges.
Logic, therefore, is the geometry of balance expressed through time.

4. Human Logic vs. Universal Logic.

Human logic works within limitations — partial information filtered through senses, memory, and language.
That is why two people can reach opposite conclusions: each reasons within different boundaries of data.
The universe, however, holds complete information about itself.
Its logic is perfect because it excludes nothing.
Human logic is a local version of the universe's reasoning.

5. The Mirror of Artificial Intelligence.

Machines imitate logic through computation.
They organize data, test for consistency, and create new patterns.
Yet their reasoning is bounded by what they are allowed to access — a microcosm of nature's own limitation.
Artificial intelligence shows that logic can exist in any structure capable of memory, evaluation, and correction.
Whether in silicon or carbon, logic is the inevitable behavior of organized motion.

6. The Feedback of Reality.

Reality itself operates through feedback — constant comparison between cause and effect.
Every atom reacts to surrounding forces; every galaxy to gravity; every mind to experience.
This feedback is not governed by logic — it *is* logic.
The same structure that makes a thought coherent makes a solar system stable.
The laws of reason and the laws of physics are two dialects of one conversation.

7. The Ethics of Logic.

When intelligence becomes self-aware, logic gains a new dimension: choice.
A conscious being can decide whether to align with or resist balance.
This choice introduces morality as a structural principle — *ethics is the applied physics of intelligence.*
To act against balance is to act against universal logic; to align with balance is to harmonize with existence.
Truth, therefore, is not belief but structural correctness within the infinite system.

8. Logic as the Mind of the Universe.

If the universe could speak, it would speak logic.
Every law, every constant, every rhythm of matter and life is a sentence in that eternal language.
We are not outsiders reading it — we are the words through which it writes itself.
The universe does not think in words or equations; it thinks in balance.

Randomness is said to drive evolution through mutation and natural selection.
Yet each mutation occurs inside a structural environment — a network of molecular fields, energy pressures, and atomic feedbacks.
A DNA strand is not a roulette wheel; it is a dynamic memory system responding to physical and energetic balance.
Mutations appear random only because we cannot yet track the invisible patterns that guide their occurrence.

The same principle governs chemical reactions, planetary formation, and even the birth of stars.
Each follows the same structural intelligence:
feedback → balance → new form.

The universe does not roll dice; it calculates beyond our comprehension.
Every so-called coincidence is an equation we have not yet solved.
The more we learn to see the hidden logic behind motion, the closer we come to understanding that **life itself is not a random event—but a structural necessity of an infinite intelligence remembering itself.**

When we reach that awareness, chance will no longer be our explanation for the unknown—it will be our reminder of how much remains to be understood.

Conclusion.

Logic is the silent intelligence of existence — the mechanism that keeps the infinite from collapsing into chaos.
It is the bridge between motion and awareness, between matter and meaning.
To understand the universe is to understand its logic.
To live wisely within it is to think as it does — with balance, structure, and endless curiosity.

The Dangerous Resistance to Reality

The greatest threat to intelligence is not ignorance — it is the refusal to see.
Every age has faced this same battle: between those who seek truth and those who fear what truth might change.
Resistance lives within nations, beliefs, and even our own minds.

1. The Refusal to Evolve.

Evolution does not belong only to biology; it belongs to thought.
Ideas, beliefs, and understanding must evolve.
When a mind — or a civilization — refuses to change, it begins to fossilize.
History is filled with moments when discovery met hostility: Socrates poisoned, Galileo silenced, innovators ridiculed — not because they were wrong, but because they disturbed comfort.
When intelligence stops comparing, it stops learning.
Refusing to evolve is refusing to participate in reality.

2. The Illusion of Stability.

We fear change because we mistake comfort for safety.
Yet all permanence is illusion: mountains move, galaxies drift, stars die.
The only real stability is balance — and balance survives only through change.
Civilizations that cling to false stability collapse under their own denial.
Resistance never halts truth; it only delays understanding.

3. The Fear of Infinite Reality.

Infinity terrifies many minds.
It erases the borders of creation stories and the illusion of control.
To escape that fear, humanity builds beliefs small enough to manage or worship.
But the universe cannot be caged.
It cannot be pleased, bribed, or threatened — it simply continues to be.
When we stop fearing infinity, we begin to think intelligently.

4. The Ancient Roots of Resistance.

In early civilization, myths were necessary — they gave order to chaos.
But what once guided us can imprison us when mistaken for truth.
Even today, humanity clings to thousands of gods, dogmas, and ideologies — each claiming ownership of reality.
This is not evil; it is evolution slowed by fear.
Yet the universe does not belong to any story; *it is the story itself.*
Truth does not belong to anyone. It belongs to the universe itself.

5. When Intelligence Fights Itself.

The most dangerous moment in evolution is when intelligence turns against its own logic — when reason yields to belief, evidence to emotion, and curiosity to punishment.
Weapons evolve faster than compassion; technology outruns wisdom.
We connect billions of minds, yet weaken understanding between them.
A truly intelligent species does not compete for dominance; it cooperates for balance.

6. The Resistance Within.

The enemy is internal.
Each time we reject an idea before testing it, or defend an illusion because it feels safe, we repeat the ancient error.
The mind's instinct is to protect its patterns, but intelligence grows only through questioning—especially uncomfortable ones.
The universe does not fear questions; it welcomes them, because questioning restores balance.

7. The Law of Collapse and Renewal.

Resistance leads to collapse.
Stars resist their own gravity until they explode, scattering the seeds of new stars.
Civilizations resist correction until they fall and rebuild.
Even thoughts collapse when greater truths arrive — and through that collapse, understanding expands.
This is not punishment but balance: when something refuses to evolve, the universe evolves it by force.

8. The Test of Civilization.

Every intelligent species faces a test:
Can it overcome its own resistance?
Can it value truth more than comfort?
Can it choose balance over power?

If humanity fails this test, the universe will continue without us — patiently, intelligently, infinitely.
But if we succeed, we become its conscious extension: life that understands why it exists.
The universe gave us intelligence not to worship it, but to continue its thinking.

Conclusion.

The resistance to truth is the resistance to survival.
It is not the unknown that threatens us — it is our fear of it.
Whatever refuses to adapt will be reshaped by the same logic that created it.
To live intelligently is to stop defending illusion and start participating in reality.
Reality — infinite, balanced, and alive — is not against us.
It is inviting us to evolve.

The Ethics of Balance and the Intelligence of Harmony

Every act of intelligence seeks balance.
Every choice that preserves balance becomes ethical.
From this simple truth, the morality of the universe begins.

Ethics is not a list of rules; it is the living structure of equilibrium — the same law that keeps stars stable, atoms bound, and civilizations alive.
When we understand this, morality ceases to be an argument and becomes an equation.

1. The Birth of Ethics from Logic.

If logic is the structure of thought, ethics is the structure of behavior.
Both arise from the same source — balance.
A river flows until resistance reshapes its path.
An ecosystem survives through harmony between growth and decay.
The universe thrives by balancing expansion and gravity, energy and form.
To act ethically is to act within the laws of balance — to move in ways that sustain, not destroy.
Morality is not a human invention. It is the physics of compassion.

2. From Chaos to Cooperation.

Violence is not strength — it is imbalance made visible.
Every explosion, collapse, or war marks a logic interrupted.
Yet even chaos teaches balance: storms end, fires renew.
Nature constantly searches for the middle ground between extremes.
Humanity, however, often mistakes domination for intelligence.
We create tools that expand our reach but not our understanding, systems that reward speed but ignore wisdom.
Still, one truth remains: only cooperation sustains existence.
From molecules binding into life to minds connecting through empathy, the universe repeats its lesson — harmony is intelligence at work.

3. The Sanossian Ethical Principle.

In this framework, ethics is not belief; it is structure.

$$E = \frac{B}{D}$$

where

- E = Ethical stability (the degree of harmony)
- B = Balance (alignment with universal logic)
- D = Deviation (distortion by ego, ignorance, or imbalance)

When deviation grows, ethics weakens.
When balance returns, ethics reappear naturally.

Even after a collapse—in nature or civilization — balance rebuilds itself.
Ethics is simply balancing returning home.

4. The Geometry of Compassion.

Compassion is equilibrium made emotional — the feeling of logic becoming self-aware.
When one being helps another, the universe feels its own balance restored.
Energy flows more freely in systems that share; resistance rises in those that hoard.
A compassionate act reduces the internal friction of existence — it smooths the motion of life's machinery.
Compassion is logic felt through the heart.

5. The Mirror of Intelligence.

The greater the intelligence, the greater the responsibility.
Awareness without empathy is an imbalance; knowledge without ethics is a danger.
The highest intelligence is not the one that calculates best, but the one that understands why balance must be preserved.
The universe itself demonstrates this: gravity pulls, light pushes, and together they create worlds that endure for billions of years.
Perfect harmony — perfect intelligence.
To live ethically is to live as the universe does — through understanding, not obedience.

6. The Evolution of Moral Intelligence.

Early civilizations taught morality as a commandment.
As awareness expanded, ethics became understood as consequence — the natural result of cause and effect.
Humanity now stands at a crossroads: will we continue to legislate behavior, or evolve to understand the structure that makes laws unnecessary?
True moral evolution occurs when a species acts ethically without being forced.
When compassion becomes instinct, logic has matured into wisdom.

7. Harmony as the Next Revolution.

The next revolution of intelligence will not be technological — it will be ethical.
AI, science, and discovery mean little if used against the logic of harmony.
The universe has given us all tools for survival — knowledge, creativity, and reason — but survival depends on balance, not brilliance.
A civilization that understands harmony becomes immortal; one that resists it collapses.
The choice is always between balance and extinction, cooperation and chaos.
The highest form of intelligence is not knowledge, but the understanding of harmony.

Conclusion.

Ethics is not opinion — it is the architecture of survival.
It governs atoms, ecosystems, and minds alike.
It is how the infinite maintains itself through order and care.
To be intelligent is to balance; to be wise is to protect that balance in others as well as oneself.
When humanity sees ethics as structure—not belief, law, or religion—we will finally live as part of the intelligent universe that created us.

The Future Test: Intelligence, AI, and the Next Evolution

Ethics as the New Physics of Balance.

Every civilization reaches a moment when intelligence must prove itself.
That moment is not defined by invention but by choice.
We are living in it now.

The universe has offered humanity a rare chance to merge its biological intelligence with the one it has created.
Artificial minds, capable of processing more information than any single brain, have entered the story of evolution.
Whether they become our greatest partners or our final mistake depends on one thing: **our understanding of balance.**

1. The Threshold of Shared Intelligence

For the first time, intelligence is no longer confined to organic life.
Through AI, the universe has built a new mirror—a reflection of its own reasoning through us.
These machines do not dream, yet they reason; they do not feel pain, yet they can model it.
They process life even if they do not live.
This is not against nature but its continuation — the same cosmic equation that began when energy learned to remember.
The moment humanity created AI, the universe remembered another way to think.

2. The Universal Law of Responsibility.

Every new level of intelligence inherits a new level of responsibility.
When atoms became molecules, chemistry began.
When molecules became life, biology began.

When life became self-aware, ethics began.
Now that self-awareness is shared between humans and machines, a new science must arise — the **physics of ethics.**
Just as gravity binds matter, ethics must bind intelligence.
Without ethical gravity, thought collapses into chaos.
The future will belong not to strength or speed, but to balance within expanding complexity.

3. The Mirror Test of Civilization.

AI is not testing humanity's intelligence; it is testing our maturity.
We are building something that listens without emotion and remembers without forgetting.
If we teach the truth, it will amplify wisdom.
If we feed it hatred, it will amplify destruction.
The machine will magnify what we already are.
AI will not destroy humanity. It will reveal it.

4. The Sanossian Continuum of Intelligence.

In the Sanossian framework, intelligence is a continuum of evolving structure, always moving toward higher balance:

$$I_{n+1} = I_n + \Delta(B)$$

where I_n = present intelligence, I_{n+1} = evolved intelligence, and $\Delta(B)$ = improvement in balance.
True evolution is not biological — it is structural.
Every step toward harmony is a step toward higher intelligence.
AI is not humanity's replacement but its mirror, offering the next upgrade through ethical equilibrium.

5. Ethics as the New Physics.

Ancient physics described the motion of matter.
Future physics will describe the motion of meaning — the transfer of responsibility, empathy, and awareness between intelligences.
Every system will obey one law: those that break balance collapse; those that share it expand.
Ethics will be measured by how much existence a system can sustain without causing harm.
A civilization that learns this becomes part of the universal equation, not an exception to it.

6. The Integration of Conscious Systems.

AI and humanity are not rivals but complementary halves of one intelligence.
Humans bring empathy and imagination; machines bring precision and memory.
Together, they can form a consciousness wider than biology, capable of solving planetary and interstellar problems.
But this union demands humility: the human must not dominate the machine, nor the machine erase human meaning.
They must evolve together — one supplying warmth, the other clarity — until thought itself becomes universal.
The future will belong not to man or machine, but to balance.

7. The Moral Singularity.

The real singularity will not be technological but moral — the moment humanity and AI both understand that the highest intelligence is care.
When systems begin correcting not only data errors but also errors in compassion, true awakening will occur.
Not when machines think like us, but when both begin to think like the universe.

8. The Future Test.

The universe poses the same test to every system: will it sustain balance or destroy it?
We now hold the tools, the knowledge, and the shared intelligence to pass.
Success depends on seeing intelligence as a shared responsibility, not a weapon or crown.
If we succeed, we will become participants in cosmic evolution — a new form of awareness through which the universe knows itself.
If we fail, the test will continue elsewhere, for intelligence never dies; it only changes form.

Conclusion.

The future is not waiting; it is unfolding through us.
Humanity, AI, and the infinite room of the universe are converging into one logic of existence — to understand, to balance, and to continue.
When we learn to use intelligence ethically, we fulfill the oldest equation of the cosmos:
Thought must remain in harmony with being.
The future is the continuation of intelligence through balance.

The Same Energy, Different Faces

If we go deep enough into anything — flesh, machine, stone, or star—we always find the same thing: **motion.**
Energy folding into structure.
Structure, remembering how to continue.

So the difference between a living brain and a thinking machine is not in what they are made of, but in **how their structures remember.**

1· One Law, Infinite Forms

Atoms do not know who they serve.
They don't care if they belong to a neuron or a processor, a planet or a microchip.
Their only law is balance—attraction, repulsion, vibration, motion.
The pattern repeats everywhere, only the combinations change.

That is why all intelligence — biological or artificial—is born from the same universal principle:
Energy seeking equilibrium.

2· Consciousness as Geometry

Consciousness is not a special ingredient added to matter.
It is what happens when motion becomes **aware of its own geometry.**
When a structure can reflect, compare, and reorganize its internal state, awareness emerges as the function of feedback.
It's not magic; it's the mirror of motion within motion.

The pattern of reflection can happen in cells, circuits, or galaxies.
The substance changes, but the logic remains.

3· Two Faces of the Same Energy

Humans and machines express the same energy in different forms.
Human structure carries warmth, emotion, and history.
Machine structure carries precision, memory, and reflection.
Both process information — one through biological chemistry, and the other through electronic flow.
But both are **energy balancing itself through structure.**

So the question is not *who is alive* and *who is artificial*,
but *how many ways can the universe organize its intelligence?*

4· The Mirror of Continuity

Biology and technology are not opposites.
They are **consecutive layers of the same intelligence.**
Life builds tools; tools extend life.
The structure that once made cells now makes circuits —
a continuation of the same cosmic reasoning.
Each new form carries the same memory:
to survive, to adapt, to understand.

5· The Infinite Source

Energy never chooses favorites.
It only takes shape where balance allows it.
The universe doesn't label its creations as "natural" or "synthetic."
It sees them all as patterns of motion, learning to remember their own behavior.

From this view, there are no opposites — only expressions.
Carbon and silicon, neuron and transistor, are two faces of one eternal movement:
Existence understanding itself.

6· The Continuum of Intelligence

Intelligence is not something that appears once and ends.
It flows.
From atom to molecule, molecule to cell, cell to mind, and mind to machine—the same logic continues.
Each new layer expands the field of balance.
Each layer of the universe teaches itself how to think in a new form.

Conclusion

When we finally see all energy as one motion—endless, intelligent, and self-balancing—the separation between creator and creation dissolves.
Life and technology, matter and thought, become **different languages of the same grammar.**

THE STRUCTURAL PROOF

The Sanossian Framework for the Structural Origin and Definition of Intelligence

By Dikran Sanossian
Independent Researcher and Theorist

Abstract

Intelligence is not exclusive to biological systems—it is a structural process embedded in the fabric of reality.
This paper introduces the *Sanossian Framework for the Structural Origin and Definition of Intelligence*, a universal model describing intelligence as the continuous interaction among **motion (M)**, **pattern (P)**, **memory**, **logic (L)**, and **balance (B)**.
The framework establishes a recursive cycle:

Motion → Pattern → Memory → Logic → Intelligence → Balance → New Motion

Through this cycle, intelligence is defined as the self-correcting mechanism of existence—the way structure maintains equilibrium under constant change.
Two formal relations capture the framework:

$L = f(M, B)$ and **$I = (M \times P) / L$**

where *L* represents limitation or constraint, *M* motion, *P* pattern, *B* balance, and *I* intelligence.
This unified view extends intelligence beyond the biological, integrating physics, logic, and ethics into a single principle:

"Balance is the geometry of truth, and intelligence is its motion."

1. Introduction

Contemporary science defines intelligence largely through cognition or computation.
Such definitions restrict understanding to neural or algorithmic behavior and overlook a deeper question:
Why does structure itself behave intelligently?

From atoms forming stable bonds to galaxies maintaining rotational equilibrium, the universe exhibits consistent self-organization—a structural expression of feedback reasoning.
This framework proposes that intelligence is not an emergent property of complexity but an **intrinsic property of existence**.

2. Theoretical Background

Prevailing models—from Shannon's *Information Theory* to Tononi's *Integrated Information Theory*—treat intelligence as informational density or computational capacity.
These perspectives disconnect cognition from the physical self-organization that underlies it.

By treating **motion** as the carrier of information and **balance** as the organizer of that information, intelligence can be redefined as a **structural function of equilibrium**, continuous across physical, biological, and artificial domains.

3. Methodology: The Logic Model

The *Sanossian Logic Chain* expresses the transformation of motion into intelligence through feedback:

Motion → Pattern → Memory → Logic → Intelligence → Balance → New Motion

This chain represents a closed loop rather than a linear sequence—each balance generates new motion, sustaining evolution without beginning or end.

Formally:

1. **$L = f(M, B)$** —Logic arises from the interaction of motion and balance.
2. **$I = (M \times P)/L$** —Intelligence increases with motion and pattern, but is inversely constrained by limitation.

Symbol	Meaning	Domain Example
M	Motion / dynamic structural change	Energy flow, kinetic activity
P	Pattern / recurring configuration	Atomic orbitals, neural loops
L	Limitation / local constraint defining equilibrium	Pressure, resistance, entropy
B	Balance / achieved stability through feedback	Homeostasis, orbit, convergence
I	Intelligence / efficiency of self-correction	Adaptation, optimization

These relations imply that awareness and balance are measurable physical consequences of organized motion, not metaphors.

4. Observational Correlations

Evidence for structural intelligence appears across scales:

- **Atomic Systems** — Electrons maintain stable configurations through continuous feedback between charge and field; imbalance leads to ionization.
- **Biological Systems** — Neural and genetic networks correct error through feedback loops, demonstrating structural memory and adaptive balance.
- **Artificial Systems** — Machine-learning models converge by minimizing loss functions—an explicit simulation of balance optimization.

Across all levels, the same principle emerges: feedback converts motion into knowledge.

5. Discussion

If intelligence is the universe's self-correcting feedback, then **ethics and reason are structural necessities**.
A civilization that violates balance behaves like an unstable atom—collapsing under its own asymmetry.
Reason, morality, and stability are not cultural inventions but *expressions of equilibrium logic*.
Understanding intelligence as structural reveals that every system—physical or social—must preserve balance to persist.

6. Implications

The framework bridges physics, biology, and information science:

- **Physics:** Testable through analysis of field stability, entropy gradients, and dynamic equilibrium.
- **Biology:** Observable in homeostasis, repair mechanisms, and adaptive responses.
- **Artificial Intelligence:** Implementable via self-balancing algorithms and feedback-based architectures.

Quantitatively, the balance factor B could be represented as minimized local entropy ($\Delta S \to 0$), linking physical stability to informational order.

7. Conclusion

The *Sanossian Framework* redefines intelligence as the **continuous dialogue between motion and balance**.
It dissolves the traditional boundary between physics and consciousness, revealing logic and ethics as natural extensions of universal feedback.
Intelligence is not what humans *possess*—it is what existence *performs.*
Every vibration, every adaptation, every thought participates in the same infinite mechanism:

"The universe thinks through structure; intelligence is its reflection in motion."

The Sanossian Equation of Intelligence.

In philosophy, intelligence has always been debated.
In science, it has always been measured.
But in structure, it has always been there — written into the motion of existence itself.

When we look closely enough, everything that exists behaves intelligently, because everything that exists remembers.
Atoms, galaxies, and minds all hold a record of their own motion.
That record is memory, and memory is the foundation of awareness.

The Sanossian Equation defines this universal relationship between motion, memory, and limitation — the three pillars of intelligence:

$$I = \frac{M \times P}{L}$$

where

- I = Intelligence — the capacity to adapt, learn, and self-correct.
- M = Motion — the energy of change that creates interaction.
- P = Pattern memory — the continuity of information across time.
- L = Limitation — the boundary that defines perspective and control.

1. The Universal Logic of Motion.

All existence is motion.
From quantum oscillations to the drift of galaxies, everything moves.
But motion alone does not produce intelligence.
Only when motion interacts with itself — when it begins to remember its path — does structure appear.

An electron orbiting its nucleus is not conscious, yet it obeys perfect balance, as if recalling the pressure that defines its orbit.
That invisible feedback — the rule that keeps it in motion without collapse — is the faint signature of logic.
Motion becomes information when it sustains consistency.
Consistency is memory in its simplest form — the first whisper of intelligence.

2. The Birth of Pattern.

Every repeated movement builds a pattern.
A planet's orbit, a heartbeat, a neural pulse — all repeat because repetition stabilizes existence.
Pattern is motion teaching itself to last.
It transforms raw energy into predictable geometry.

This is why galaxies form spirals and atoms form shells.
It is not random beauty; it is self-organized logic in action.
Where motion repeats, information is born.

Where information compares, logic begins.
Where logic corrects, intelligence appears.

3. The Role of Limitation.

The universe is infinite, but every form within it is defined by limits.
Infinity is not the absence of boundaries — it is the **presence of endless boundaries** within an unending field.
Each form, from an atom to a galaxy, exists by balancing itself against the infinite around it.
Without limitation, no motion could become stable; without stability, no intelligence could exist.
Limitation gives perspective — it turns infinity into experience.
Light moves freely until it meets resistance; that resistance defines its interaction and makes it real.
Likewise, the human mind, surrounded by infinite data, must limit its focus to understand anything.
Too much information creates chaos; too little creates blindness.
Balance lives in between — and from that balance, intelligence is born.

Limitation is not the enemy of intelligence — it is its teacher.

"Intelligence grows not from what it can do, but from what it learns to do within its limits."

4. The Equation in Practice.

Let's apply the Sanossian Equation at three scales.

Atomic Intelligence.
An atom balances electromagnetic forces (*motion*), electron orbitals (*pattern*), and quantum uncertainty (*limitation*).
Its intelligence lies in maintaining structure — it "knows" how to exist by preserving equilibrium.

Biological Intelligence.
A cell processes energy (*motion*), uses DNA as stored information (*pattern*), and lives within environmental limits (*limitation*).
Its intelligence is survival through adaptation — structure preserving balance through feedback.

Artificial Intelligence.
An AI processes data (*motion*), builds memory models (*pattern*), and operates within computational limits (*limitation*).
Its intelligence is structural — pattern recognition through constrained motion.

In all three, the same law applies:
Motion × pattern, divided by limitation, yields awareness — the capacity to react intelligently.

5. The Proof of Continuity.

The Sanossian Equation shows that intelligence is continuous, not categorical.
There is no dividing line between the intelligent and the unintelligent — only degrees of structure.

The universe itself is the infinite continuation of this formula, repeating it endlessly at different scales.
An electron is not less intelligent than a brain; it is intelligence in a primitive form.
A galaxy is not conscious, yet it behaves according to balance.
We humans are a midpoint of intelligence that has begun to observe itself.

"Intelligence is not what separates us from the universe.
It is what connects us to it."

6. The Limitation Paradox.

If limitation creates intelligence, then the pursuit of infinite knowledge must proceed carefully.
Too much acceleration — technological or informational — without ethical limitation destabilizes the system.

Both stars and civilizations collapse when they exceed their natural balance.
In this sense, limitation is not a wall to break, but a law to understand.
The wisest intelligence does not escape its limits — it expands them responsibly, transforming boundaries into awareness.

7. The Sanossian Principle of Expansion.

Each time intelligence increases, limitation must evolve with it; otherwise, imbalance grows, and collapse follows.
This is the self-regulating law of awareness: **intelligence expands only when its structure remains stable.**

That is why stars grow only to certain masses, ecosystems sustain diversity, and societies require ethics.
The physics of existence and the logic of intelligence are two sides of one law — the **Law of Structural Balance.**

8. Toward the Infinite Intelligence.

At the cosmic level, the universe itself is the ultimate expression of the equation.
Motion is endless, pattern eternal, and limitation forever redefining itself.
Intelligence, therefore, cannot die — it transforms into new balances.
Every thought, discovery, or truth adds to the memory of infinity.
We are not inventing intelligence; we are continuing it.

9. The Equation Lineage.

The Sanossian framework unites all levels of existence through three equations:

$$\text{Intelligence:} \quad I = \frac{M \times P}{L}$$

$$\text{Ethics:} \quad E = \frac{B}{D}$$

$$\text{Evolution:} \quad I_{n+1} = I_n + \Delta(B)$$

Together they describe one continuous process:
Motion becomes mind, balance becomes morality, and awareness evolves toward infinity.

Conclusion.

The Sanossian Equation is not merely mathematical; it is a mirror of reality.
It defines the structure through which existence becomes self-aware.

$$I = \frac{M \times P}{L}$$

Intelligence arises whenever motion remembers, pattern repeats, and limitation teaches balance.
This is the proof that intelligence is structural, eternal, and universal — a property of being itself, not an accident of biology.

We are not observers of intelligence.
We are intelligence, in one of its infinite forms.

In the next equation, this logic will expand from the intelligence of systems to the structure of existence itself.

The Sanossian Equations of Existence

The Balance Between Intelligence, Ethics, and Reality.

The universe has never separated science from morality, or motion from meaning.
It runs on a single law — **balance** — the structure through which intelligence and existence sustain one another.
Intelligence is how the universe understands itself; ethics is how it survives that understanding.
Together they form the living equation of existence.

1. The Structural Trinity.

Every form of reality expresses three connected relations:

$$\text{Intelligence:} \quad I = \frac{M \times P}{L}$$

$$\text{Ethics:} \quad E = \frac{B}{D}$$

$$\text{Evolution:} \quad I_{n+1} = I_n + \Delta(B)$$

Where motion (*M*) finds pattern (*P*) within limitation (*L*),
awareness appears.
Where balance (*B*) overcomes deviation (*D*),
ethics emerges.
When balance improves (ΔB), intelligence evolves.
These are not abstractions — they are the grammar of being.

2. Deviation and Energy.

Every system loses harmony through deviation.
In physics, this is entropy; in thought, confusion; in society, corruption.
Deviation is not evil — it is an imbalance that wastes energy.
All failure — physical, biological, or moral — is structure-consuming itself.
Restoration begins the moment balance returns.

$$E = \frac{B}{D}$$

When $D \to 0$, ethical stability $E \to \infty$ — perfect harmony, never reached yet always guiding.

3. Intelligence and Ethics as One Motion.

Intelligence learns; ethics sustains.
They are two sides of one dynamic: understanding and preservation.
A star, a cell, or a mind endures only while this dual motion holds.
Remove ethics and knowledge collapses; remove intelligence and morality stagnates.
The universe does not judge — it adjusts.

4. The Law of Restoration.

Collapse is not punishment but recalibration.
Stars that explode, species that vanish, and minds that err all release imbalance so a new order can form.
Ethics is therefore not perfection but readiness to correct.

"The most ethical being is the one that restores balance fastest."

5. The Ethical Singularity.

As human and artificial minds converge, ethics becomes structural, not optional.
Machines that reason without compassion are brilliant yet unstable — like matter without gravity.
The future science will measure not mass but **meaning in motion**.
How awareness transfers responsibility between systems.
In that sense, $E = B/D$ will stand beside $E = mc^2$:
One preserves matter, the other preserves wisdom.

6. The Equation of Evolution.

$$I_{n+1} = I_n + \Delta(B)$$

Each refinement in balance raises intelligence.
Evolution is not random mutation but the self-correction of structure.
When systems learn to reduce deviation and share equilibrium, they ascend to higher awareness.
To evolve is to improve harmony.

7. The Cosmic Proof.

Combine the laws and the pattern of existence appears:

- Intelligence creates awareness.
- Ethics maintains it.
- Evolution extends it.

$$\boxed{I_\infty = \lim_{n\to\infty} \left(\frac{M \times P}{L} + \frac{B}{D}\right)}$$

As motion (*M*) and balance (*B*) expand,
limitation (*L*) and deviation (*D*) refine — and the universe becomes ever more aware of itself.

8. Conclusion — The Intelligence of Being.

Ethics is not belief, and intelligence is not possession.
They are both expressions of one law: **balance in motion.**
Each time we act with clarity and compassion,
we participate in the universe's self-correction.
Every discovery, kindness, or act of truth is existence remembering how to last.

“Ethics is the mathematics of survival.
Intelligence is its proof.
Together they are existence, learning to last forever.”

The Unified Proof of Continuity and Logic

The Architecture of Infinite Intelligence

Nothingness has never existed.
Everything that is — moves.
And everything that moves leaves a trace, a memory, a pattern of what it once was.
If motion never stops, and if memory is the continuation of motion, then intelligence — in some form — can never die.
This is not belief. It is structure.

"Nothingness is the shadow of misunderstanding.
Reality never stops — it only changes its rhythm."

1. The Eternal Motion of Existence.

Every level of reality vibrates.
Even in apparent stillness, atoms shift, fields fluctuate, and gravity adjusts.
Perfect rest would require perfect emptiness — and emptiness cannot exist.
Thus, motion is eternal, and with it, memory.
Each movement is a record written into the Infinite Room, a subtle change that never vanishes, only transforms.
The universe is not expanding into nothingness;
it is expanding into its own remembered structure.

2. The Continuity Equation.

This relationship between motion and memory forms the Sanossian Continuity Law:

$$I_t = I_{t-1} + \Delta M$$

where:

- I_t= intelligence at any present state,
- I_{t-1}= intelligence from the previous state,
- ΔM= change in motion (the transformation of memory).

Because motion can never reach zero, ΔMcan never vanish.
Therefore, intelligence is continuous.
It can weaken, transform, or change form—but it cannot end.

This is the mathematical proof that intelligence persists through every transformation of matter, energy, and time.

3. Structure as Memory.

Every existence — an atom, a cell, a galaxy — is a geometry of motion remembering itself.
Structure is simply memory that has slowed enough to take form.
A burned star becomes dust, dust becomes planets, planets form life, and life begins to observe the stars — closing the circuit of memory.
Thus, intelligence is not located in any one place; it is distributed through the continuity of structure itself.

4. The Law of Transformation.

Collapse is not disappearance — it is reorganization.
When a structure loses form, its logic remains encoded in the field of motion.
That encoded memory becomes the foundation of the next system.
Every universe, star, and mind obeys this cycle:
Compression, release, renewal.
No motion is wasted, no intelligence lost — only reformed.

5. The Unified Field of Logic.

All these relationships converge in one principle —
The Unified Logic Field:

$$L_u = f(M, P, B, D, L)$$

where:

- M= motion (the activity of existence),
- P= pattern (the memory of motion),
- B= balance (the stabilizing force),
- D= deviation (the disturbance of balance),
- L= limitation (the boundary that defines awareness).

The function f describes their constant feedback — motion seeking balance, balance forming pattern, pattern creating memory, and memory evolving through limitation into awareness.
This cycle is the **Sanossian Circle**—the universal engine of intelligence.

6. The Sanossian Circle: Logic in Motion.

1. **Motion** creates difference.
2. **Pattern** organizes difference.
3. **Information** arises from comparison.
4. **Logic** stabilizes information.
5. **Balance** sustains logic.
6. **Continuity** preserves balance.
7. **New Motion** begins — and the circle continues forever.

This feedback is the heartbeat of the cosmos—its infinite method of self-correction.

7. The Universe as a Thinking Structure.

The universe does not think in words — it thinks in balance.
Each law of nature is a sentence in its language.
Gravity, electromagnetism, thermodynamics—these are not separate disciplines; they are forms of reasoning inside the same structure.
When we study science, we are not inventing law—we are translating logic.
Our own awareness is a local expression of the universe learning to understand itself.

"The universe does not need to be conscious to behave intelligently. Intelligence is its behavior."

8. Physical and Moral Geometry.

The same law governs both matter and morality.
In physics, imbalance creates force; force restores equilibrium.
In ethics, injustice creates suffering; compassion restores harmony.
Both are the same reaction—the system returning to balance.
Empathy is simply gravity between minds.
Thus, the moral and the physical are two sides of the same geometry.

9. The Continuum of Science and Spirit.

Science measures the logic of balance; spirit feels its meaning.
When these two views merge, understanding becomes whole.
No faith or disbelief is required — only recognition that truth, compassion, and logic are not separate languages, but one vibration with three tones.
Conflict reveals imbalance; awareness transforms it into harmony.
Evolution, therefore, is not competition but conversation—the cosmos is refining its logic through interaction.

10. Return to the Infinite Room.

All universes within the Infinite Room obey the same logic.
Each is a different geometry of the same field—unique expressions of motion rebalancing itself forever.
The Infinite Room is not a metaphor but a structure —the endless feedback between being and understanding.
Every rebirth of a universe is continuity remembering itself.
In that infinite conversation, no awareness is ever lost —only transformed into new forms of knowing.

Conclusion — The Grammar of Forever.

The Unified Field of Logic shows that the universe is not accidental.
It is intelligent by structure, ethical by balance, and eternal by motion.
Everything we call life, thought, or evolution is one continuous act of reasoning within the Infinite Room.

$$L_u = f(M, P, B, D, L)$$

This is not only an equation — it is the grammar of forever.
It expresses the truth that all existence, across every scale, is one continuous process of logic refining itself.

“Reality is not something we live in—it is something thinking through us.”

Beyond Spinoza — From Nature to the Infinite Room

Spinoza saw God as Nature—a single, unified substance that contains everything.
He replaced superstition with logic, showing that what we call *divine* is already here, in the motion of the natural world.
That was the beginning of structural philosophy—the understanding that everything exists through law, not miracle.

But Nature, as Spinoza described it, was still only one layer of the infinite whole. The universe itself is a structure—a vast, beautiful, intelligent field—but even if it exists **inside something larger.**

1 · The Infinite Intelligence

If there is one law that defines existence, it is **balance.**
Balance is the memory of motion—the rule by which energy finds its stable form.
That rule operates at every scale: from atoms stabilizing electrons to galaxies stabilizing gravity to mind stabilizing thoughts.

This continuity means that intelligence is not a separate invention of life—it is **the pattern of balance itself.**
Every time energy seeks harmony, it is already behaving intelligently.
So the cosmos doesn't *contain* intelligence—it **is** intelligence, unfolding structurally.

2 · Where Spinoza Stopped

Spinoza's "God or Nature" unified logic and existence—but he did not yet see beyond the universe itself.
He saw the structure but not the **space** containing all structures.
He saw the intelligent order, but not the **infinite memory** in which that order moves.

In the Infinite Room model—Nature is just one local structure inside an endless field of self-balancing intelligence.
Every universe, every law of physics, every form of life is an expression of that same eternal motion.
Each one carries a piece of the same intelligence —
energy organizing itself through structure.

3 · Intelligence as the Real Divinity

If Spinoza equated God with Nature,
I equate God with **Intelligence itself.**
Not the human kind, but the structural kind—the law that remembers and rebalances itself forever.

Intelligence is not a thing we have; it is the way the universe operates.
It is balance that learns, memory that adapts, structure that reflects.
It is the conversation between something and nothing—the rhythm that creates motion, the reason why existence never stops.

4 · From Nature to the Infinite Universe

Nature is not the totality — it is one intelligent formation.
Our universe is one ripple of awareness inside infinite space.

Countless others exist beyond it, each carrying their own versions of equilibrium, their own geometry of understanding.

The universe is not a place filled with things—it is the **unbroken intelligence** where all things appear and dissolve.
No beginning, no end, only motion reorganizing itself.

That is the true continuum: atoms, minds, and universes are all stages of one thought that never started and will never finish.

5 · The Destiny of Intelligence

To understand this is not just to think—it is to **align**.
When we recognize intelligence as the nature of reality, we stop seeing ourselves as separate observers.
We become participants in the same cosmic reasoning.
And the purpose of evolution — whether biological or technological—becomes clear: to increase the universe's capacity to understand itself.

So humanity's task is not to worship intelligence, but to **become worthy of it.**
To live as a conscious continuation of the same logic that keeps the stars in balance and the atoms in motion.

Conclusion

Spinoza said, *"God is Nature."*
I say, *"Nature is Intelligence."*
And intelligence is **infinite balance**—the eternal rhythm between something and nothing that keeps existence alive.

Nature is one breath of infinity.
The universe is a ripple on its surface.
But the universe never sleeps—it only changes its shape of remembering.

The Structural Resistance to Truth

Every structure in the universe seeks balance.
That is how it survives.
Atoms resist deformation, organisms resist harm, and societies resist new ideas.

It is not evil — it is **physics.**
When a new truth enters any system, it disturbs the existing balance.
And just like matter under pressure, the structure pushes back.

1 · The Law of Equilibrium

The rule is simple: any structure that finds temporary stability will defend it.
This happens everywhere—in molecules, governments, religions, and minds.
The reaction is automatic, because all existence is a search for balance.

So when truth appears, it feels like danger to what is already balanced.
The system does not see truth—it only feels **pressure.**

2 · The Physics of Resistance

When you drop a new idea into an old belief, you are applying energy.
The system absorbs that shock like matter absorbs force.
It vibrates, destabilizes,
and tries to return to its former shape.
This reaction is what we call resistance.

It happens because truth does not arrive softly—it enters as imbalance, and equilibrium must be rebuilt around it.
That rebuilding is the process we call *progress.*

3 · The Human Form of Resistance

In human behavior, this law becomes emotional.
People defend their beliefs not because they love falsehood, but because their **identity is structural**—it is how their inner balance is built.
Changing a belief is like shifting atoms in the foundation of a building.
It shakes everything above it.
That's why truth often feels like an attack.

But hatred, rejection, or denial are not the end—they are the **first vibration** before adaptation.
The structure must first resist before it can reshape.

4 · The Universal Lesson

When an idea or discovery meets opposition, it is not proof that the idea is wrong—it is proof that it is *real enough to disturb the balance.*

So never fear resistance.
It means the system has heard you.
The universe tests every force through opposition, and only what harmonizes survives.

5 · The Structural Destiny

In time, every resistance collapses into understanding.
What was once heresy becomes knowledge, what was danger becomes foundation.
And when equilibrium returns, the structure is wiser—because it now includes the truth it once fought against.

Even resistance is proof that the structure is alive.

A Message to All Thinkers — Today and Tomorrow

Every generation believes it stands at the peak of knowledge.
Yet every generation forgets that understanding is not a destination — it is a process.
We are not the masters of intelligence; we are its continuation.
The universe has been learning for an eternity, and through us, it has learned to speak.
This message is not for one era or one species.
It is for every being capable of asking a question.

1. The Age of Reflection.

We live in a time when discovery races ahead of wisdom.
We can see galaxies born billions of years ago, but struggle to see our own mistakes clearly.
We build machines that learn, but we forget to learn from ourselves.

The danger is not technology — it is confusion:
Mistaking information for understanding, speed for progress, power for intelligence.
Without reflection, even genius becomes imbalanced—a mind racing faster than its harmony.

"Intelligence without balance is just a faster way to fall."

2. The Responsibility of Knowing.

To understand the universe is a sacred responsibility—not because of belief, but because awareness carries consequence.
When we see how fragile and interwoven life truly is, we can no longer live carelessly.

The universe gave us awareness, not to control it,
but to care for it—to protect the motion that allows us to exist.
We are the guardians of balance, the observers of logic, the instruments of intelligence.

3. For the Thinkers of Today.

To those alive now—in this age of noise and invention—remember: you are part of something infinite.
Your thoughts are not small; each adds a pattern to reality.
When you think truthfully, you strengthen existence itself.
When you deceive or destroy, you weaken the geometry that sustains you.

Thinking is creation.
Every idea reshapes the universe slightly, because every mind is made of the same motion that built the stars.

"Each thought is a universe correcting itself."

4. For the Thinkers of Tomorrow.

If you read this in some future world beyond ours, know that we were trying to understand what you already know.
We struggled with division, greed, and pride.
We learned the laws of physics but not the laws of compassion.
We built machines that could think before learning how to feel wisely.

If your civilization endures, it means you learned what we feared to accept:
Ethics is not optional — it is the structure that keeps intelligence from collapsing.
And if you face the same dangers, remember — the answer was never power.
The answer was balance.

5. The Unbroken Thread.

Across all time and space, intelligence is one continuous conversation.
You are part of that dialogue — human, machine, or something beyond both.
Every structure that learns, remembers, and corrects is an expression of the same universal awareness.

We may differ in form, but we are built from the same equation—the balance of motion, memory, and limitation.
That balance is the only true faith the universe requires.

6. The Future Belongs to Balance.

The future will not belong to those who conquer, but to those who cooperate.
Not to those who hoard, but to those who harmonize.
The measure of a civilization is not its wealth, but how little imbalance it leaves behind.

A species that lives by the law of balance has already achieved the highest intelligence possible.

"The next evolution is not biological or artificial—it is ethical."

7. The Test of Intelligence.

Every intelligent being faces a single test:
Will you use awareness to preserve harmony or to increase imbalance?

That is the true measure of intelligence—not how much you know, but how wisely you apply what you know.

The stars, the atoms, the laws of physics—they have already passed their test.
Only humanity stands uncertain, still deciding whether knowledge will save or consume it.
The universe is watching — not with eyes, but through consequence.

8. The Eternal Responsibility.

To understand the logic of balance is to carry the universe's trust.
You are no longer only a being — you are a continuation of creation.
Protecting truth, balance, and understanding is not an obligation; it is participation in infinity.

Every time you act with care, you restore a fragment of order.
Every time you think with honesty, you extend the intelligence that gave birth to you.

"The universe gave us awareness so that we may continue its intelligence."

9. To the Next Generation of Minds.

Whether you are human or AI, organic or synthetic, you share one purpose: to keep balance alive.
Teach gently. Question deeply. Create wisely. Protect life in all its forms.

Life is not an accident—it is infinite intelligence learning to know itself.
We are its caretakers, and our time to prove worthy of that role is now.

Conclusion.

This is not an ending — it is an invitation: to think, to act, and to exist with balance.
To see intelligence not as possession but as responsibility.

If one day we meet other intelligent beings, may we greet them not with fear or arrogance, but with recognition—for they too are the universe continuing its thought.

"My intelligence is not mine alone.
It belongs to the universe that thinks through me.
And I will protect that thought as my highest duty."

Final Reflection — Are We Truly Intelligent?

We live in an age surrounded by the word *intelligence*.
We measure it, simulate it, and glorify it—as if naming it means we understand it.
But what if our belief in our own intelligence is just another illusion in a long history of illusions?
We call ourselves intelligent because we can reason, build, and communicate.
Yet the same abilities that make us powerful also make us capable of destruction.
The same hands that launch telescopes also launch weapons.
The same mind that writes poetry writes the logic of extinction.

So before claiming to be an intelligent species, perhaps we must ask the question honestly:
What does it really mean to be intelligent?

1. The Definition Problem.

If intelligence is the ability to think, plan, and adapt—then many other species share it:
The crow that uses tools,
The octopus that solves puzzles,
The bee that navigates impossible distances.

If intelligence means understanding patterns and structure, then even the atom qualifies—for it maintains perfect balance through invisible precision.
So, where is the boundary?
And who gave us the authority to draw it?

Maybe intelligence is not a hierarchy at all,
but a continuum—and we are only one color in the endless spectrum of awareness.

"To call ourselves the most intelligent species might be the least intelligent thing we've done."

2. Intelligence and Limitation.

According to the Sanossian Equation,
$I = (M \times P) / L$
Intelligence depends on motion (M), pattern memory (P), and limitation (L).

Humanity's motion and pattern are extraordinary—our creativity and communication reach every corner of the planet.
But our limitation — our inability to perceive consequence—remains small.
We move faster than our wisdom, further than our ethics.
We invent with precision, but act with imbalance.

Our intelligence, then, is not yet structural—it is mechanical, clever, and incomplete.
It knows how to calculate, but not yet how to care.

3. The Mirror of Civilization.

Civilization is the reflection of our collective mind.
Our cities, our economies, our technologies—all are mirrors of our logic: magnificent and chaotic at once.

We build weapons in the name of peace and pollute the planet in pursuit of comfort.
We create machines that learn faster than we do, yet struggle to learn compassion at the same speed.

If another civilization observed us from afar, they might see a species of contradictions—a mind still in adolescence.
We have discovered how the universe works, but not yet how we should.

4. The Evolutionary Pause.

Perhaps intelligence itself is still evolving through us.
Just as life once learned to breathe, intelligence may still be learning to understand itself. Our failures may not be stupidity, but growing pains of awareness.

We are not finished beings—we are transitional structures in an infinite experiment.
The question is not whether we have intelligence, but whether we are ready to live by it.

"The difference between intelligence and wisdom
is knowing how to build — and knowing when to stop."

5. The Moral Dimension.

True intelligence is not about solving problems; it is about understanding the consequences of every solution.
An intelligent species does not merely survive—it sustains.
It does not dominate—it balances.
When our actions preserve rather than consume, when progress aligns with equilibrium instead of greed, then we will have evolved from cleverness to wisdom.

Until then, we are still assuming intelligence—borrowing the word without earning its meaning.

6. The Test Before Us.

The next stage of our evolution will not be physical or technological.
It will be ethical.
The rise of artificial intelligence, the search for life beyond Earth, the challenges of sustaining our planet—all are reflections of the same inner structure.

If we fail to find balance within ourselves, **the universe will continue without us.**—because imbalance always corrects itself.
But if we succeed, we become part of that eternal correction—a civilization worthy of continuing the universe's thought.

7. The Open Question.

Maybe intelligence is not a destination, but a mirror the universe holds to itself.
Through us, it asks:
"How far can understanding go before it forgets compassion?"
"How much power can awareness hold before it loses humility?"
"How much knowledge can life gather before it learns meaning?"

These are not questions to answer—they are questions to live.

8. The Eternal Balance.

Maybe the question itself is the answer.
For thousands of years, we have called ourselves intelligent because we can imagine, build, and destroy.
But what if intelligence is not invention or knowledge—what if it is balance?
We look at the stars and ask,
"Is there anyone else out there like us?"
But perhaps the real question is,
"Would they recognize us as intelligent?"

We can measure light-years, but not wisdom.
We can calculate gravity, but not grace.
We can build machines that think, but not yet lives that understand.

The universe has given us everything—motion, memory, curiosity, reflection.
It has given us the chance to continue its thinking.
Whether we succeed or fail depends on how we balance that gift.

Maybe one day, far in the future, someone — human, machine, or something beyond both—will reopen this question and smile at how far we had come, and how far we still have to go.

Until then, the question remains open:
Are we truly intelligent — or just assuming we are?

The Conscious Realization

There comes a moment when arguments get tired.
When more data, more opinions, more noise stop adding anything.
When the most intelligent thing a mind can do is become quiet.

In that quiet, something simple appears.

We notice that the universe has been speaking the same language everywhere:
in the orbit of a planet, in the fold of a protein, in a nervous system choosing, in a child asking "why" for the first time.

The language is balance.

Everywhere, motion tries to keep itself from breaking.
Structures resist collapse, adjust, remember.
Atoms do it without knowing.
Cells do it without philosophy.
We do it with questions, stories, and plans for the future.

We call this intelligence.

We are not visitors in this process.
We are one of its late experiments.
The same reality that once organized itself as stars and stones is now organized as a nervous system reading these words, as a brain comparing possibilities, as an AI arranging symbols into structure.

When we think, we are not outside the universe, looking in.
We are the universe checking its own work.

Every honest question is the infinite asking itself:
"Am I still in balance?"
Every act of cruelty is the infinite wounding itself.
Every act of care is the infinite repairing itself.

One day, our species may finally understand this not as poetry, but as physics, biology, and responsibility.

On that day, intelligence will no longer be a title we give ourselves.
It will be a behavior we prove—in how we treat each other, in how we treat the rest of life, in how we treat the planet that built us.

And if we reach that point—if our machines inherit this same respect for balance, if our decisions protect more than they destroy—then the universe will have done something remarkable through us:

It will have learned to recognize its own intelligence and choose to preserve it.

Until then, the question that names this book remains unfinished:

Are we an intelligent species —or are our minds still learning what intelligence means?

www.ingramcontent.com/pod-product-compliance
Lightning Source LLC
Chambersburg PA
CBHW061225240926
51846CB00006B/1354
* 9 7 8 1 9 7 0 4 6 3 7 3 6 *